Gracious Me!
Exploring God's grace and what it means to be gracious

LEA EPPLING

Gracious Me!
Exploring God's grace and what it means to be gracious
by Lea Eppling

Published by BKM Resources
ISBN 978-1-939283-11-5

© Copyright 2019 Lea Eppling.

All rights reserved. No part of this book may be reproduced or transmitted in any form or by any means, electronic or mechanical, including photocopying and recording, or by any information storage or retrieval system, without the written permission of the author or publisher.

Unless otherwise noted, Scripture quotations are from the Holy Bible, New International Version®, copyright © 1973, 1978, 1984 by International Bible Society. Scripture quotations identified HCSB are from the Holman Christian Standard Bible®, copyright © 1999, 2000, 2002, 2003, 2009 by Holman Bible Publishers. Scripture quotations identified NASB are taken from the NEW AMERICAN STANDARD BIBLE®, Copyright © 1960,1962,1963,1968,1971, 1972,1973,1975,1977,1995 by The Lockman Foundation.

Printed in the United States.

5411 Lawson Rd.
Gainesville, Georgia 30506

BKM Resources is a division of Bucky Kennedy Ministries

To my husband, David, for his continual encouragement. And to my children, Abby and Andrew, for allowing their lives to be used as living illustrations of God's grace. Thank you for loving me, even when I'm ungracious.

Acknowledgments

My appreciation to my mom, Sandra, for teaching me to be a student of Scripture and for advising me on how to teach God's Word effectively. I also owe a debt of gratitude to my editor and friend, Thelma, whose knowledge and insights are invaluable. Thank you both for modeling what it means to be gracious.

Contents

Foreword 6

Introduction 7

Using This Study 8

Session 1
Grace 11

Session 2
Worship 21

Session 3
Choose 39

Session 4
Speak 55

Session 5
Give 73

Session 6
Forgive 95

Epilogue 111

End Notes 115

Foreword

When it comes to those who impart spiritual truths, there are two kinds of people. Allow me employ an analogy for each. First, there is the spiritual travel agent. This person makes recommendations based on her study of various destinations. No previous travel experience is required; just a working knowledge of the accommodations and routes to get there.

On the other hand, there is the spiritual tour guide. This person doesn't just tell you how to get somewhere, she leads you down a path she's already explored. She has experienced the journey, is familiar with the winding roads, and has discovered the best places to stop along the way. She has not only studied the route; she has traveled it personally. Lea Eppling is a spiritual tour guide.

Gracious Me is the product of the grace road Lea has traveled. It's a practical itinerary for a trip she's already taken—a trip she wants you to experience with her. And as you'll see, receiving and giving grace is a lifelong journey. This is an adventure that does not end until we see the One whose merit has made this grace available. So, get ready. You're about to be blessed on this trip!

Anthony George
Senior Associate Pastor
First Baptist Atlanta

Introduction

Am I gracious? That was the question on my mind as I began a personal study of the word grace in Scripture. The Holy Spirit began to convict me that rather than being a conduit of God's grace, I had become a grace hoarder. I selfishly accepted God's grace (in many ways) but failed to be gracious with others, often holding the people around me to an impossible standard. I observed older godly women and desired to be like them, but I also realized that I wouldn't just suddenly wake up one day and be gracious! This was going to take work. That was the beginning of a simple, personal prayer, "Lord, help me to be a more gracious woman."

When I was approached about speaking at a weekend retreat I asked, "Can we talk about grace?" God used my preparation for that weekend to turn my personal study of His grace into more than I could have imagined then. This study reflects my journey to be a more *Gracious Me!*

My prayer is that this study will leave you with a sense of awe at the wonders of God's grace. Will you choose a time and place right now to complete your daily study? Determine to set aside at least 15 minutes a day to dig into God's Word and learn how He has been, and continues to be, gracious to you. Then join me in this simple prayer, "Lord, help me to be a more gracious woman."

Using this study...

We'll begin this six-session study by gaining a basic understanding of God's grace before exploring more deeply how God is gracious with us. We'll then turn our attention to what it means to be gracious in three specific areas – speaking, giving, and forgiving. Each session is divided into a daily study, a group discussion, and a lesson.

The daily study contains five days of homework for each session. You'll notice that there's not much commentary in the daily study. Its purpose is to guide as you dig into Scripture related to each week's topic. You'll then get together one day a week for a group discussion from the daily study. Each group can decide how long the discussion lasts, but keeping it to approximately 30 minutes seems to work best. Of course, your discussion time will be most profitable if everyone in the group has completed the daily study. By thoughtfully and prayerfully completing each day's assigned work, you'll have more to contribute to the discussion than just your initial thoughts on a passage or concept.

The final component to each session is a lesson on that week's topic. The subject matter will be the same as the daily study, but it will usually cover a passage in Scripture other than what you've already studied during the week. Or, it will delve deeper into a passage that was introduced during the week. The lesson can be taught in a group setting or read individually prior to the discussion. Either way, a lesson guide is provided for individual note-taking.

By no means is this an exhaustive study of God's grace; we can only scratch the surface. That's why I hope you'll pay attention to the sources cited at the end of the book. The commentaries I chose make it easier for non-scholars (like me) to glean more information. Investing in a good study Bible is the best way to get started.

Gracious Me!

Session 1

Grace

Session 1
Grace: Guide

Grace: how God freely demonstrates His goodness to humankind, though we're undeserving of His goodwill.

Main Thought: The quality of graciousness starts with an inward realization of God's grace that results in a new outward reality.

A Great Need	Isaiah 6:1-8

God's holiness requires atonement for sin.

Recognize Who God is (v3).

Recognize who I am (v5).

Recognize what He did (v7).

Life Principle: A skewed view of God results in an unrealistic view of myself and of my need for His grace.

| A Gracious Plan | Romans 5:8 and Ephesians 2:8-9 |

The greatest expression of God's grace toward humankind is His gift of salvation.

Life Principle: I can't truly be gracious unless I've first received God's gracious gift of salvation.

| A Godly Life |

Growing in grace results in a gracious and godly life.

Know (James 4:6)

God's grace continues in the life of a Christian, providing what we need to speak and respond in a godly way.

Grow (2 Peter 1:3-8; 3:18)

Growing in the grace of Jesus Christ is allowing God to continually mold us into the image of His Son. However, spiritual growth is not automatic; it requires effort on our part.

Flow (1 Peter 4:10-11)

Life Principle: God's grace is continually available to me and should continually flow through me.

The Bottom Line

God desires that we become conduits through whom His manifold grace can grow and flow.

Session 1
Grace: Lesson

My initial desire to be more gracious came from observing women who seemed to say and do the right thing at the right time and in the right way. However, those women were more than courteous and well-mannered - they were godly. You see, you can be taught how to behave properly, but being gracious is about more than outward behavior. Genuine graciousness comes from the inside out and is generated by God's grace.

What exactly is grace? Most commentators agree that grace is the unmerited favor of God. It's how He freely demonstrates His goodness to humankind, though we're undeserving of His goodwill. Although every person receives some measure of God's grace (Psalm 145:8-9; Isaiah 26:10), it is God's saving grace that can transform us into gracious women.

Main Thought: The quality of graciousness starts with an inward realization of God's grace that results in a new outward reality.

A GREAT NEED
Isaiah 6:1-8
God's holiness requires atonement for sin.

Isaiah 6 offers a clear picture of our need for God's saving grace by painting a stark contrast between God and humankind. While it's true that God is a loving Father, He is also the holy, holy, holy…Lord Almighty. His holiness indicates His purity. The repetition of the word holy in Isaiah 6:3 emphasizes His total separation from sin. We live in a culture that wants the benefits of a heavenly Father's favor and goodwill without recognition of what His absolute holiness requires – atonement, repentance, and obedience.

Seeing God for Who He is gave Isaiah amazing clarity about himself. His sinfulness, as well as that of his nation, was unbearable in contrast to the righteousness of the Lord God Almighty. Isaiah's confession brought forgiveness (removal of guilt), mercy (not receiving what is deserved – Romans 6:23), and grace (receiving what was not deserved).

> *"The worse we realize we are, the greater we realize God's grace is. Never believe anything about yourself or God that makes His grace to you seem anything less than astonishing. If trying to comprehend it doesn't stretch your brain, you just aren't getting it."*[1] – Randy Alcorn

Like Isaiah, we need to come to the place of complete transparency before God by acknowledging our sinful state and how it has prevented us from living in a manner worthy of God's calling. We don't need to dwell on past sin, but we do need to have an Isaiah 6 moment, when we recognize the holy God Who mercifully and graciously provided the payment for our sins. When you grasp Who God is and see yourself from Isaiah's perspective, then you're willing to say, "Here I am" to whatever assignment He gives, no matter how challenging. (Later in this session, we'll discuss the role of God's grace in facing challenging situations.) God has revealed Himself through His Word. How much time do you set aside each day to read it in order to know Him better? When is your time to get alone in the presence of God?

Life Principle: A skewed view of God results in an unrealistic view of myself and of my need for His grace.

A GRACIOUS PLAN
Romans 5:8 and Ephesians 2:8-9
The greatest expression of God's grace toward humankind is His gift of salvation.

A widely used acronym for grace is: God's riches at Christ's expense. Try to wrap your mind around the fact that the holy Son of God died for sinful people. Since we cannot live up to the standard that His holiness requires, He graciously provided a way at Calvary. God's favor toward us is not based on anything we do or don't do, but is based completely on His love, mercy, and grace.

Have you received His gracious gift of salvation? Then, this is where we have to get brutally honest with ourselves. We admit that we can't meet the standards of God's holiness by our own merit, and we gratefully accept His grace. Yet we often require the people in our lives to live up to our expectations.

That's hoarding grace! Respect may be earned, but grace is an undeserved gift.

Life Principle: I can't truly be gracious unless I've first received God's gracious gift of salvation.

A GODLY LIFE
Growing in grace results in a gracious and godly life.

Know - James 4:6
Accepting God's gracious gift of salvation requires humbly acknowledging who we are – sinners without hope of helping ourselves. God's grace continues in the life of a Christ follower, providing all that we need to speak and respond in a godly way until we're home with Him.[2] You've probably watched a mature believer remain steady and composed when faced with an overwhelming challenge and thought, "I could never handle that situation the way she did." Here's what you need to know: He gives us more grace. It's what we do with that grace that determines whether or not we're gracious.

Grow - 2 Peter 3:18 and 2 Peter 1:3-8
Many of us have become quite good at the second part of this verse: grow in knowledge. We listen to sermons and attend Bible studies that fill our heads with information about God and Scripture. However, when growing in knowledge isn't balanced with growing in grace, a prideful and judgmental attitude usually develops. Growing in the grace of Jesus Christ is allowing God to continually mold us into the image of His Son.[3] Although God has provided everything needed for our sanctification, spiritual growth is not automatic – it requires effort.

You grow in the grace of the Lord Jesus Christ as you diligently increase in these qualities.[4] The result is a godly life. The nature that you nurture becomes your natural response. When my son learned to play tennis, he struggled with his serve. His coach had him perform the service motion over and over again without the ball. He practiced it so many times that his muscle memory eventually took over. Serving became more instinctual than intellectual – a reflex rather than a forced motion. That's the picture of diligently pursuing Christ. As you're molded into the image of Christ, responding as Jesus would respond becomes the reflex – because you're allowing His divine nature to respond in and through you.

Flow - 1 Peter 4:10-11
This passage specifically addresses the use of spiritual gifts (abilities given to believers by the grace of God), which are meant to benefit the body of Christ. As members of a church use their various spiritual gifts to serve one another and to teach biblical truth, God's grace flows in its various forms through them to the other members (1 Corinthians 1:4-7). May I suggest that if you are not using your spiritual gift(s) in your local church body, then you are hoarding God's grace? Using what God has given to you for the benefit of others is being gracious. We are mere stewards of God's favor and goodwill.

God's grace also has various forms just as we face trials of various kinds (1 Peter 1:6). His grace is multi-dimensional, so it can meet every need, which means you'll never face a situation that God's grace can't cover. Through the years I've learned that grace holds my hand and walks with me through difficult situations when I rely on God's Word and respond in God's strength (v. 11).

> *"Christians are a lot like tea bags; we're worth more after we've been through hot water." – Jerry Vines*

We miss so much by asking God to remove a painful situation instead of asking for the grace to face it. No woman enjoys labor pains, but the pain of labor eventually gives way to the joy of new life. As my kids were growing up, we talked about the events of the day they were born. I wanted them to know their stories. Now, no birth story is truly complete without talking about how many hours of labor we endured, but that was never my focus in telling my kids their birthday stories. The pure joy of holding that newborn gift of God made it worth every minute. What situation is challenging you to birth stronger faith?

> *"My grace is sufficient for you, for my power is made perfect in weakness." Therefore I will boast all the more gladly about my weaknesses, so that Christ's power may rest on me.*
> *- 2 Corinthians 12:9-10*

His grace is sufficient! There is unbelievable strength in relying on His grace. And there is often unimaginable joy after the most intense spiritual labor pains (James 1:2-5). That's when you have a story of grace to tell. However, we must experience God's grace during the challenging moments of life before we can share it. How would relying on God's grace in your present circumstance allow you to be a conduit through which grace flows to others?

It's interesting that both 2 Peter 3:18 and 1 Peter 4:11 end with giving glory to God. Being gracious is ultimately about glorifying God – telling your stories of how God has graciously seen you through. I'm afraid that most Christians are more concerned with how God can help them than how they can glorify Him. This study isn't a self-improvement course on how to be a better person; it's about experiencing and extending God's grace each and every day. As we do that, He is honored and glorified.

Life Principle: God's grace is continually available to me and should continually flow through me.

Will you allow this study to be for you what it's been for me – a thorough self-examination, allowing God to show you where you might be hoarding His grace?

The Bottom Line

> *God desires that we become conduits through whom His manifold grace can grow and flow.*

Gracious Me!

Session 2

Worship

Session 2
Worship: Daily Study

Main Thought: God graciously gave us through Jesus what could not be achieved by obeying the Law.

DAY ONE: The Breadth of the Law

In order to better understand the depth of God's graciousness to us we need to look at what life was like under the Old Testament system of law. The Old Testament Law was divided into three categories: civil, moral and ceremonial. Each category served a specific purpose. But which of these laws are believers today obligated to obey? Why did the New Testament church seem to abandon much of Israel's law? Today we'll compare the first two categories, look at the differences between them, and explore their current relevance.

Civil Law

1. Civil laws guided Israel's relationships with one another as citizens. Although it's impractical to follow many of these laws specifically today, the principles behind them are the foundation of Judeo-Christian life.[1] Read Deuteronomy 24:10-22 and identify examples of Israel's civil laws.

    - Verses 10-13 deal with _____ made from one neighbor to another.

    - The ethical nature of how employers treat _____ is addressed in verses 14-15.

    - Verse 16 emphasizes personal responsibility for one's _____.

    - The care of _____ is addressed in verses 17-22.

2. How can one or more of these examples guide your behavior this week?

Gracious Me!

Moral Law

Of all of Israel's laws you are probably most familiar with the laws given in Exodus 20:1-17. These direct commands of God still apply today - not as a means of salvation, but they reveal how a believer's life can please and honor God.[2] Write each command in your own words.

Our Relationship with God	Our Relationships with One Another
1)	5)
2)	6)
3)	7)
4)	8)
	9)
	10)

What do you learn about the nature and will of God from The Ten Commandments?

DAY TWO: The Burden of the Law

Today, we'll explore the last category of Israel's law and see the burden associated with living up to the letter of the Law.

Ceremonial Law

1. Israel's ceremonial laws were part of their worship and were designed to point God's people to the Messiah, Jesus Christ. These laws weren't needed after Jesus' sacrifice on the Cross.[3] Scan the chapter headings in Leviticus 1-6 to find the names of the five offerings Israel made regularly and fill in the left side of the chart following.[4]

Session 2: Worship

Name of the Offering	Components of the Offering	Purpose of the Offering
Leviticus 1	A young bull; male sheep or goat; dove or pigeon - without defect	Atonement for sin
Leviticus 2	Fine flour and oil; unleavened cakes and wafers; new grain	Gratitude for God's provision
Leviticus 3	An animal without defect from the herd or flock	Worship and thanksgiving to God; fellowship meal with family
Leviticus 4 – 5:13	Varied: young bull, goat or lamb without defect; two doves or pigeons; fine flour	Atonement for specific, yet unintentional sin
Leviticus 5:14-6:7	A ram without defect	Atonement for sins against another person; restitution for the person wronged

2. How do you see Jesus Christ pictured in one or more of these offerings?

3. Use Galatians 3:10, 23; James 2:10

   a. What one word from each passage describes the burden of living under the Law?

   b. Choose one word from your answer in 3a. How have you personally been released from this burden?

Gracious Me!

DAY THREE: The Limitations of the Law

Worshipping under the Law was burdensome. Yet it still couldn't fully accomplish what was needed. Let's examine the limitations worshippers faced living under law.

1. Next to each verse below, write what could not be gained by observing the Law.

   Romans 3:20a

   Galatians 2:16

   Galatians 2:21

   Galatians 3:2

2. Write the definition of the following:

   Righteous

   Justified

3. Look at Galatians 2:16 and Romans 3:24 together. How is justification accomplished?

4. Which part of living under the reign of grace are you most thankful for today?

DAY FOUR: The Purpose of the Law

So what's the point? If the Law had to be kept perfectly and couldn't provide righteousness or justification, why did God give it in the first place? God has a design and purpose for everything He does. Today we'll take a look at three main purposes of the Old Testament Law.

Session 2: Worship

1. Use the verses below to fill in the blanks.

    a. Romans 3:20b and 7:7

    Purpose 1: The Law gave an awareness of _____.

    b. Leviticus 1:3-4; Galatians 3:19

    Purpose 2: The Law offered temporary _____ because of _____ until the coming of _____.

    c. Galatians 3:24-25

    Purpose 3: The Law pointed to _____ as the only perfect sacrifice.

2. Galatians 3:24-25 mentions that the Law was in charge, acting as a guardian (HCSB) or tutor (NASB). What lessons have you learned by studying the Law this week?

DAY FIVE: The Fulfilling of the Law

Yesterday, we saw that God had distinct purposes for giving the Law. Today's study is the hinge that swings us from living under the reign of law to living under the reign of grace. Let's look at how God fulfilled the Old Testament Law.

1. It's important to understand that grace wasn't "Plan B." Fulfilling the Law through grace was always God's plan.

    a. How does 1 Peter 1:18-20 prove this point?

b. What elements of the Law do you see in these verses?

2. How was the Law fulfilled according to Acts 13:38-39 and Romans 10:4? From each verse, write one thing that Christ offered that the Law could not.

3. Read Romans 8:1-4. What do you learn about:

    a. Christ Jesus

    b. Those who are in Christ Jesus

4. What past sin still brings you a feeling of condemnation? From what past or present sin do you need to be reminded that you have been set free?

Session 2
Worship: Guide

Main Thought: God graciously gave us through Jesus what could not be achieved by obeying the Law.

The Purpose of the Law	Hebrews 10:1-4

The Law was intentionally designed to prepare God's people for the Messiah.

    Pointed to Christ

    Taught the Futility of Human Effort

    Brought an Awareness of Sin

    Offered Temporary Atonement

Life Principle: Only the blood of Jesus Christ can take away our sin.

The Limitations of the Law	Hebrews 10:1-2, 11

The Law could not take away our guilt or make us right with God.

    Guilt Remained

    No Righteousness or Justification

Life Principle: It's only by the grace of God that we can have a right relationship with God.

The Fulfillment of the Law	Hebrews 10:5-14

Fulfilling the Law through grace was always God's plan.

    Jesus, Our Sacrifice

Jesus, Our High Priest

Life Principle: God's grace allows me to stand before Him free of guilt and shame.

The Results of Grace	Hebrews 10:15-18

God established a New Covenant, removing the need for further sacrifice.

The New Covenant

Complete Forgiveness

Life Principle: Jesus' sacrifice moved us from law to grace; from death to life.

The Bottom Line

We cannot become gracious until we first accept God's awe-inspiring grace.

Session 2

Worship:Lesson

Hebrews 10:1-18

When I began to explore what the Bible says about God's grace, the New Testament writers kept pointing back to the Old Testament laws of Israel. Pretty soon I understood why. In order to grasp what God's grace accomplished at Calvary, we need to understand what it was like to be a worshipper under the ceremonial laws of Israel.

Main Thought: God graciously gave us through Jesus what could not be achieved by obeying the Law.

THE PURPOSE OF THE LAW

Hebrews 10:1-4
The Law was intentionally designed to prepare God's people for the Messiah.

Pointed to Christ

Hebrews 10:1 says that the Law is only a shadow. Think of it this way: the shadow of your hand on a doorknob will never open the door because the shadow has no physical matter with which to grab the knob. However, the shadow can demonstrate how to open the door even though it doesn't have the ability to perform the act. The Law demonstrated what only Jesus Christ could accomplish. The entire sacrificial system pictured what Jesus would do when He died on the Cross.

> *"The shadow of a key cannot unlock a prison door;*
> *the shadow of a meal cannot satisfy a hungry man;*
> *the shadow of Calvary cannot take away sin."*[5] – John Phillips

Taught the Futility of Human Effort

Hebrews 10:1 points out the constant repetition of the sacrifices of God's people. Just as children learn through repetition, God was reiterating to His children that no effort of their own could give them a right standing with

Him. Even the most earnest of worshippers couldn't attain the perfection that God's holiness requires. The sacrificial system of the Old Testament taught generation after generation that God's favor could not be bought or earned. Salvation came through a Savior as a gift of grace, not by the works of human hands. Isn't it comforting to know that God's love and grace aren't based on anything that we do? Our obedience pleases God, but it does not earn us points toward His favor or affection.

Therefore the Law has become our tutor to lead us to Christ, so that we may be justified by faith. –Galatians 3:24 (NASB)

Brought an Awareness of Sin
The Day of Atonement was an annual reminder of the cost of their sin[6] (Hebrews 10:3). Because the life (blood) of an innocent animal was required as payment, they had to feel the weight of their offenses toward God. The Law made them conscious of their sin (Romans 3:20).

Offered a Temporary Solution
But it was impossible for the blood of animals to take away sin. Even though the sacrificial system was God's provision for their past sin, it couldn't atone for the sins of the next day or the day after that. God fulfilled His promise to forgive sin even though sacrifices couldn't remove it.[7] The Law was a temporary system of atonement with a temporary solution for sin.

What then was the purpose of the law? It was added because of transgressions until the Seed to whom the promise referred had come.... – Galatians 3:19

Life Principle: Only the blood of Jesus Christ can take away our sin.

THE LIMITATIONS OF THE LAW
Hebrews 10:1-2; 11
The Law could not take away our guilt or make us right with God.

Guilt Remained
Why would an Israelite who just offered a sacrifice in

worship still feel guilty? Because the Law couldn't cleanse them perfectly; otherwise the need for sacrifices would have ended. So then, let's follow this train of thought to its natural conclusion. Since Jesus, the Lamb of God, was the perfect sacrifice, why would you or I as His followers still feel guilt after confessing a particular sin? Satan tries to use guilt to stop us in our tracks. Guilt is just the awareness of sin as a fact (feeling the weight of our sin), whereas conviction is the prompting by the Holy Spirit to repent and change. Guilt tries to convince you that you can't possibly serve God; conviction leads to repentance and correction so that you can serve God.

No Righteousness or Justification

This week's daily study encouraged you to become more familiar with the words righteousness and justification in order to understand why they couldn't be accomplished under the Law. Righteousness is "the character quality of being right or just."[8] Since God alone is inherently righteous, it's impossible to be right with God by our own merit. Justification is a legal term picturing the believer's new righteous status before God.[9] Let that last sentence sink in for a moment – the guilty are now without guilt!

I do not set aside the grace of God, for if righteousness could be gained through the law, Christ died for nothing!   *– Galatians 2:21*

Know that a man is not justified by observing the law,
but by faith in Jesus Christ. So we, too, have put our faith in Christ
Jesus that we may be justified by faith in Christ
and not by observing the law, because by observing the law
no one will be justified. – Galatians 2:16

Life Principle: It is only by the grace of God that we can have a right relationship with God.

THE FULFILLMENT OF THE LAW
Hebrews 10:5-14

Fulfilling the Law through grace was always God's plan.

Jesus, our Sacrifice

The death and resurrection of Jesus replaced the Old Covenant (the Law) with the New Covenant (grace). Because He embodied everything that God intended from eternity past, His perfect single sacrifice makes us holy. Even though we're guilty, through Christ we are justified and seen as righteous. Imagine that you're in bankruptcy court, deeply in debt and still accumulating more debt. The judge is about to make his ruling on your case when a wealthy benefactor walks into the courtroom and pays your debt in full. Now you're in right standing with the judge. He declares you to be innocent. That's exactly what we have in Christ! He has taken your judgment and paid your sin debt in full.

Jesus, our High Priest

Jesus offered one sacrifice for all sin for all time, and then He sat down at the right hand of the Father. This would have especially caught the attention of the religious crowd since the work of priests was never finished (continual sacrifices). But because of Christ's "better" sacrifice, He could declare from the Cross, "It is finished" (John 19:30). The Law is fulfilled, and God sees believers just as He sees His Son – holy and perfect.

> *Therefore, there is now no condemnation for those who are in Christ Jesus, because through Christ Jesus the law of the Spirit of life set me free from the law of sin and death. For what the law was powerless to do in that it was weakened by the sinful nature, God did by sending his own Son in the likeness of sinful man to be a sin offering. And so he condemned sin in sinful man, in order that the righteous requirement of the law might be fully met in us, who do not live according to the sinful nature but according to the Spirit. – Romans 8:1-4*

You and I can go to one of two extremes: 1) rationalize and excuse certain sins thinking, "Well, nobody is perfect"; or 2) beat ourselves up long after the fact, asking forgiveness over and over for the same sin. I struggled with guilt for years due to a period of rebellion against God as a young adult.

The guilt actually lasted much longer than the rebellion did! I couldn't get over the disappointment in myself because my focus was on my imperfection.

"No condemnation" means there is no judgment for the guilty.[10] Jesus provided what the Law could not: justification; the guilty become righteous, innocent before God. That was my standing with God as a child when I chose to follow Christ, and it was my standing after I repented from my rebellion as a believer (1 John 1:9). However, guilt over my sin blinded me to the fact that "innocent" is different from "not guilty." God didn't forgive me because there was a reasonable doubt; all evidence of my guilt has been removed! The promise in Romans 8:1 is a picture of God's grace – giving us what we don't deserve.

Life Principle: God's grace allows me to stand before Him free of guilt and shame.

THE RESULTS OF GRACE
Hebrews 10:15-18

God established a New Covenant, removing the need for further sacrifice.

The New Covenant
The presence of the Holy Spirit in our lives is evidence that we have a right standing with God. This New Covenant was established by Christ's blood, not the blood of goats and lambs. It is written on the hearts of Christ's followers, not on stone tablets. Having God's law in your mind means you can know God's will. His law in your heart gives you a desire to do His will. The presence of the Holy Spirit in your life gives you the power to follow God's will.

Complete Forgiveness
Under the New Covenant, sins are not simply covered, they are gone. God knows our every thought and every action. He sees the ugliness in the depths of our hearts, and yet He promises to forgive and forget when we confess those things to Him. Are you living as a prisoner to something in your past? God didn't put those shackles on you – you did.

I can tell you from personal experience that His sacrifice is enough. His grace is enough!

Life Principle: Jesus' sacrifice moved us from law to grace, from death to life.

I remember exchanging texts with my mom one morning after spending hours studying what you've just read. My only thought was, "Wow!" She texted back, "Wow is worship." Are you at "Wow" yet? Are you as overwhelmed by God's grace as I was that morning? You and I have the privilege of approaching God in worship from this side of the Cross. We can see how God's gracious plan has unfolded, and I'm in awe.

The Bottom Line:

We cannot become gracious until we first accept God's awe-inspiring grace.

Gracious Me!

Session 3

Choose

Session 3
Choose: Daily Study

Main Thought: The cost of being gracious is dying to our own desires and choosing to live for God's desires.

DAY ONE: The Gift of Grace

Last week, we studied what life was like under the Law. Session two moved us from the reign of law to the reign of grace. This week we'll gain a greater appreciation of God's grace by looking at what it cost Him to secure our salvation through His Son, Jesus Christ.

1. What do you learn from Hebrews 2:9-18 about:

    Jesus

    Believers in Christ

2. Using your answers from question #1, which fact about Jesus is the most awe-inspiring? What gift to believers humbles you? Why?

3. Verse 9 declares that salvation is offered to everyone by grace. What was the cost?

DAY TWO: Crucified with Christ

Our salvation came at great cost: the life of Jesus. If extending grace to humanity was costly to God, then it stands to reason that it will cost us something to be gracious. The first step is to recognize what has already happened within you as a believer, and then choose to live within that reality. Let's explore what it means to be crucified with Christ. Read Romans 6:1-11.

1. From Romans 6:5-7, name things that take place in the life of a person *united* with Christ.

2. What phrase from Romans 6:6 is repeated in Galatians 2:19-21?

3. In your own words, what does it mean to be crucified with Christ?

4. Below are a few things a person no longer has or needs when he or she dies physically. How would being dead to your old self affect how you act and relate in the following areas?

    Pride

Comforts

Schedule

Rights

DAY THREE: Dying to Self

Yesterday, we learned that followers of Jesus are crucified with Christ. The power of sin is broken and we are no longer in slavery to it. Yet we each wrestle with our sin nature. We must choose daily to live according to our new nature, not the old. We'll spend the next two days exploring the principle of dying to self.

1. Read Luke 9:22-24. What does Jesus tell His disciples will happen to Him?

2. What three instructions are given to a disciple of Christ in verse 23?

3. What did a cross signify to the disciples and the people of that day? (See John 19:17-18.)

4. With question three in mind, what do you think it means to take up (your) cross daily?

5. In what specific area of your life do you need to deny (your)self and follow Christ?

DAY FOUR: Dying to Self

In John 12:23-33 Jesus predicts His death and gives a powerful word picture about dying to self: a grain of wheat doesn't produce more seed until it falls to the ground and dies. Jesus chose to give His life as a sacrifice for sin, making it possible for us to become children of God. Likewise, followers of Christ are dead to their former self and are most productive when they choose to live for God's purposes rather than their own.

1. Read John 12:23-33. In your own words, what does Jesus say in verse 25? How do you relate it to a kernel of wheat falling to the ground to die? (Also see Luke 9:24.)

2. John 12:27-28 shows that Jesus was fully aware of what He would suffer in order to fulfill His Father's will. What two prayers were possibilities for Jesus and which did He choose?

3. Living for God's purpose means seeking to glorify Him in every situation. What difficult circumstance have you been praying to be removed from your life? How could God be glorified by your choice to die to self regarding the matter?

DAY FIVE: Asserting Your Rights

Dying to self often means giving preference to someone else's desires over our own, but it doesn't always mean giving way to more forceful personalities. Jesus was meek, not weak. There are times when it's okay to assert your rights. The best example of this in Scripture is the Apostle Paul. Let's look at when and why Paul asserted his rights.

1. Read Acts 22:22-23:11. What claim did Paul make that changed his standing? What did the Lord tell Paul would be the result?

2. Paul asserted his rights when it furthered the cause of Christ. What rights do you have that can further the work of Christ?

3. What area of your life needs to be rendered dead to self?

4. How can you make Philippians 1:20-21 a reality in your life this week?

Session 3
Choose: Guide

Main Thought: The cost of being gracious is dying to our own desires and choosing to live for God's desires.

Know the Facts	Romans 6:1-10

Jesus' death, burial and resurrection replaced the power of sin with the power to live for God's purposes.

    We are dead to sin.

    We identify with Christ.

    We are freed from sin.

Life Principle: As a follower of Christ, the only power sin has over me is the power I give to it.

Act on Faith	Romans 6:11

In Jesus we are dead to sin and free to live completely for God.

Gracious Me!

Life Principle: The key to facing temptation successfully and responding graciously is to act in faith on the facts of Scripture.

Make a Choice	Romans 6:12-23

Grace draws us to yield to God as our loving Master, not to the desires of our sinful nature.

Choosing to Obey

    1) Because of Grace

    2) Because of the Master

    3) Because of the Results

Life Principle: Whatever I yield to will become my Master.

The Bottom Line:

Everything we need to live a godly and gracious life has already been given to us.

Session 3
Choose: Lesson

Romans 6

When I told my husband that we were expecting our first child, he hyperventilated. He literally had to breathe into a paper bag. He continued to be petrified throughout my pregnancy, but a sudden and drastic change took place the first time he held her. The facts he knew in his head became reality in his hands, and he named her Abigail, which means "joy of the Father."

You see, we can know something as absolute fact, but choosing to act on it changes everything. Romans 6 shows us how knowing, acting, and choosing are part of becoming more gracious. Future lessons will discuss how to be gracious, but first we need to understand the personal cost of choosing to become a conduit of God's grace.

Main Thought: The cost of being gracious is dying to our own desires and choosing to live for God's desires.

KNOW THE FACTS
Romans 6:1-10

Jesus' death, burial, and resurrection replaced the power of sin with the power to live for God's purposes.

We are Dead to Sin
The first verse of Romans 6 presents us with a great question: Is grace a license to sin? There's no doubt that many people view God's grace as a sort of get-out-of jail-free card. How can that be, seeing that verse two says that we have died to sin? I don't believe this is promoting sinless perfection. It's about choosing who controls your thoughts and actions. Willful sin takes advantage of grace. Just as a literal dead body is unresponsive, you can choose to be unresponsive to sin. Think of a situation you need to avoid because it sets you up to sin. What guardrails do you need to put into place to protect your mind and heart from that sin?

We Identify with Christ
In His death...

This week's daily study explored what it means to deny yourself, take up your cross, and follow Christ (Luke 9:23-24). Although you may have heard someone attribute their "cross" to a difficult situation or an individual, the meaning was clear to Paul's Roman audience. A cross symbolized death. Jesus said that in order to be His follower, one must willingly die to self-interest. The daily study also asked you to consider that when someone dies physically, that person no longer has things such as pride, a schedule, comforts, or rights. In other words, being crucified with Christ means you no longer push a personal agenda; you allow God to interrupt your day as He sees fit, and you're willing to put yourself in uncomfortable situations if it means you can impact others for Christ. We must deny anything in ourselves that isn't Christ-like. Only in Jesus can death really mean life.

I have been crucified with Christ and I no longer live, but Christ lives in me. – Galatians 2:20a

> *"The true expression of Christian character is not good doing, but God-likeness. If the Spirit of God has transformed you within, you will exhibit Divine characteristics in your life, not good human characteristics. God's life in us expresses itself as God's life, not as human life trying to be godly. The secret of a Christian's life is that the supernatural becomes natural in him as a result of the grace of God, and the experience of this becomes evident in the practical, everyday details of life."[1] - Oswald Chambers*

Do you remember the WWJD craze several years ago? We don't have to wonder, "What would Jesus do?" when faced with a difficult situation because His Spirit indwells you as His follower. We just have to get out of the way and let Him live through us. Trying to act godly, in human terms, is exhausting, but letting Jesus be Jesus in and through you is liberating!

In His burial...

If you've been baptized by immersion, then your pastor might have said something like, "Buried with Christ in death and raised to walk in the likeness of Christ." Going under the water symbolizes that you have done spiritually what Christ did physically. Baptism is symbolic of leaving the old person – the person you used to be – dead and buried. Willful disobedience to God and His Word is the spiritual equivalent of digging up a dead body!

In His resurrection...

We'll be united with Jesus in resurrection after death, but we have resurrection power now.[2] If Jesus has the power to conquer sin and death, then He certainly has the power to guide, provide, and help us overcome temptation. Living in the power of Jesus gives us the ability to be gracious. So are you living in the power of His resurrection, or are you dragging a dead body around?

> *I want to know Christ and the power of his resurrection and the fellowship of sharing in his sufferings, becoming like him in his death, and so, somehow, to attain to the resurrection from the dead. –*
> *Philippians 3:10-11*

We are Freed from Sin

The Cross of Jesus Christ is our emancipation from slavery to sin. Before Christ we were controlled by our sinful nature, but Jesus conquered sin and death on the Cross. We cannot miss the importance of verse 10. Jesus not only died for sin, He died to sin – breaking its power.[3] Don't be surprised when those outside of Christ habitually sin – the old nature is their way of life. Believers, however, have been set free. Although human nature is the explanation for our sinful choices, it's not a valid argument for sin in the life of a child of God because we have the power to do otherwise.

***Life Principle:** As a follower of Christ, the only power sin has over me is the power I give to it.*

ACT IN FAITH
Romans 6:11
In Jesus we are dead to sin and free to live completely for God.

If you have given your life to Christ, then you are dead to sin, and you now have the power to live and respond just as Jesus would. Living in that actuality requires putting your faith into action. The word, "count" in verse 11 means to reckon, which is an accounting term indicating a deposit into an account.[4] Imagine that a multi-millionaire opened a bank account in your name, giving you access to his wealth. Just believing that the money was in the account wouldn't change your life until you acted on it by going to the bank and claiming it. Similarly, we are to claim our death to sin in Jesus. If you believe that you are really dead to sin, then act in faith.

> *Put to death, therefore, whatever belongs*
> *to your earthly nature... – Colossians 3:5*

Romans tells us that we are dead to sin, and Colossians says we have to put our sinful nature to death. Both are true. We're dead to sin in Christ, yet we wrestle with our sin nature every day. Acting in faith is the hinge between simply knowing that you're dead to sin and making it a reality. We often fail to grasp the value of our faith in connection with God's grace. You may not feel dead to a particular sin, but believing in faith that God says you are dead to it allows you to claim that truth as fact. Do you have a habitual sin? If you belong to Jesus, then you have died to that sin in Christ – you don't have to live in it any longer! He has deposited untold spiritual wealth into your account, but you must choose to access all that He has provided.

Life Principle: The key to facing temptation successfully and responding graciously is to act in faith on the facts of Scripture.

MAKE A CHOICE
Romans 6:12-23 and Romans 12:1-2
Grace draws us to yield to God as our loving Master, not to the desires of our sinful nature.

While it's possible for followers of Christ to sin, it's not inevitable. We can choose not to give in to the desires of our sinful nature.

When the Apostle Paul explains "offer your body" in the above passage, it's interesting that the only part of the body he specifically mentions is the mind. Your mind determines who you are and who you will become. Your attitudes and behaviors will fall in line with what you choose to think about. What kind of thought life do you currently have? How does what you feed your mind match up to God's standards?

> *Finally, brothers, whatever is true, whatever is noble, whatever is right, whatever is pure, whatever is lovely, whatever is admirable – if anything is excellent or praiseworthy – think about such things. – Philippians 4:8*

Rather than offering our minds and bodies to sin, Paul urges us to offer them to God as instruments of righteousness (Rom. 6:13). Our bodies are God's dwelling place, but they are also tools He can use to build His kingdom. In the past week, how were your words and reactions instruments of God's grace? Paul gives three reasons to offer ourselves to God rather than to sin.

The first reason is that we are under grace, not law. We have moved from slavery (sin and the law) to submission (grace) (vv. 14-15). Grace should compel us to obey, not give us an excuse to sin. We should also obey God and His Word because we have a new Master (vv. 16-20). If Jesus is your Savior, then shouldn't He also be your Lord and Master? The words "Lord" and "no" simply don't go together. Take a moment to examine whom or what you are submitting to. In the past week, did you give in to a temptation of your old nature, or did you overcome by yielding to Jesus as your Lord and Master?

> *"Who is to be first, myself or God? That decision decides all other decisions."[5] - Selwyn Hughes*

Finally, we should choose obedience to God because of the results (vv. 21-23). Under our old master (sin), the payment was death – eternal separation from God. But our new Master (Christ) graciously offers freedom, holiness, and eternal life.[6] What results are you getting? Eternal life through the saving knowledge of Jesus Christ is wonderful, but there's so much more to the Christian life than waiting for Heaven. There is freedom in submission to the Lord Jesus. He knows how to meet our needs and desires better than we do. Satan is an expert in the art of deception. He will appeal to your old nature by marketing sin as a way to gratify a desire – even a good desire. If he can convince you that grace gives wiggle room to sin, then he can divert you from a fruitful, free, and holy life. God's grace empowers you to yield to Christ instead of yielding to sin.

> *For the grace of God that brings salvation has appeared to all men. It teaches us to say "No" to ungodliness and worldly passions, and to live self-controlled, upright and godly lives in this present age." - Titus 2:11-12*

Life Principle: Whatever I yield to will become my Master.

There's one more thing I don't want you to miss. Read back through Romans 6 and underline the past tense verbs throughout the chapter. Paul isn't describing what we will be some day; he is telling us what we already are in Christ. Now that you know the facts, will you put your faith into action and choose to live in the reality that you are dead to sin and alive to God? Will you live in the freedom of God's grace?

Bottom Line

Everything we need to live a godly and gracious life has already been given to us.

Gracious Me!

Session 4

Speak

Session 4
Speak: Daily Study

Main Thought: Words have consequences and reveal the true nature of the person speaking.

DAY ONE: Controlling the Tongue

Nothing reveals more quickly whether or not we're gracious than when we speak. Words are extremely powerful. What you say and how you say it can change the course of your life as well as the lives of others. The first step to more gracious speech is to get our tongues under control. Today's study, from James 3:1-5a, will help us to focus on who is in control of what we say.

1. According to verse 2, mature Christians keep their tongues under control, which leads to what?

2. Who is in control of the bit and the rudder? In your own words, how is your tongue like a bit and a rudder?

3. Give an example of how the direction of your life has been affected, positively or negatively, by something you have said.

4. In what specific situation do you need to keep your tongue under control this week? Stop now and ask God for help, submitting your words to His control.

Gracious Me!

DAY TWO: Using Restraint

Our mouths are out of control when we don't exercise restraint over what we say. Yesterday, we saw how James illustrated restraint by picturing a rider holding the reins to the bit in a horse's mouth. Today we'll look at why restrained speech is so important.

1. James 3:5-6 describes a mouth that is out of control. In these verses the tongue is compared to a wildfire. What similarities can you think of between the damage caused by a wildfire and unrestrained talking?

2. Using the Proverbs listed, write what you learn about the following:

   a. Proverbs 10:19 - The result of too much talking

   b. Proverbs 10:19 – The result of self-control and restraint

   c. Proverbs 17:27-28 – Characteristics of a restrained mouth

   d. Proverbs 13:3; 21:23 – The result of a guarded mouth and tongue

e. Proverbs 29:11 – Foolishness versus wisdom

3. Which of the Proverbs from today's study caught your attention the most? Why?

DAY THREE: Learning to Listen

Yesterday, we discussed using restraint with our words. People who don't use restraint when talking are often poor listeners. Let's keep exploring Proverbs to see what we can learn about being better listeners.

1. To whom does Solomon urge the reader to listen in Proverbs 22:17-18? What piece of wise, godly counsel have you received and how have you applied it to your life?

2. What does Proverbs 25:12 say we should accept from a wise person? Put the result in your own words.

3. Use Proverbs 15:31-33 to give the results of the following actions:

    Listening to a life-giving rebuke

Ignoring instruction

Heeding correction

Fearing the Lord & having humility

Notice the progression from hearing to heeding. Hearing may bring knowledge but applying knowledge brings wisdom. We can read the Bible our entire lives and not become wise. We must listen and then act on what we've heard.

4. On the scale below, rate yourself as a listener. Be honest.

1   2   3   4   5   6   7   8   9   10

5. The art of listening starts with asking questions rather than talking about oneself. To whom do you turn for wise counsel? Think of at least one question you would like to ask that person and record it below. Jot down the day and time this week that you might have opportunity to ask for advice or counsel.

Session 4: Speak

DAY FOUR: Removing and Replacing

The Bible has a lot to say about what we say. Certain language, tones, and attitudes need to be removed from our speech in order to avoid hypocrisy. Today we're going to explore the principle of remove and replace.

1. Fill in the chart below for each passage listed. Find what should be removed from our speech and what it should be replaced with. What is the result of removing it or not removing it? Notice what character traits each passage encourages you to pursue.

Remove	Replace	Result	Character Traits
Psalm 15:1-5			
			• Loyalty • Truthful • Honest • Trustworthy
Proverbs 15:1-4			
			• Honest • Encouragement • Compassion • Patience • Gentleness
Ephesians 4:29			
			• Encouragement • Sensitivity

2. Look up "deceive" in a dictionary. In your own words, explain the difference between lying and deceiving.

Gracious Me!

    3. Honesty and truthfulness are the opposites of deceit and lies. What does 1 John 3:18 have to say regarding these traits?

    4. What would it look like if Psalm 35:28 was a reality in your daily life?

DAY FIVE: Finding the Source

If you treat only the symptoms of a physical illness, you will continue to deal with the problem. Your doctor, however, can prescribe medication or treatment to resolve the issue at its source. Now apply that principle to what we've learned this week about the words we use. Have you ever made a sudden negative or biting comment and thought, "Where did that come from?" Well, the negative comment was just the symptom of a deeper issue. You have to deal with the source of the problem in order to make a significant change in what you say and how you say it. Let's start by looking at what Jesus said about the origin of our speech.

    1. What did Jesus say about the natural state of your heart in Matthew 15:10-20? What symptoms of this heart problem have you noticed in your own speech?

    2. In contrast to Matthew 15:19, what kind of heart does Proverbs 22:11 describe? What accompanies this kind of heart and what is the result?

3. Read Colossians 4:6.

   a. What do you think it means to let your conversation be full of grace, seasoned with salt?

   b. What instructions in verse 2 help us accomplish gracious speech?

4. Write Psalm 19:14 as a personal prayer regarding your speech.

Gracious Me!

Session 4
Speak: Guide

Main Thought: Words have consequences and reveal the true nature of the person speaking.

Giving Up Control	James 3:1-5a

A spiritually mature woman places her tongue under God's control.

Life Principle: My words will not reflect God's grace unless I give Him control of my tongue.

Damage Control	James 3:5b-8

An uncontrolled tongue has the power to damage and destroy.

    Fire

    Poison

Life Principle: Words spoken in the heat of the moment or in self-defense are seldom gracious.

Session 4: Speak

| Quality Control | James 3:9-12 |

Praising God but then engaging in gossip, slander, or criticism is abnormal.

    Avoid Hypocrisy

    Unnatural

Life Principle: A hypocritical, inconsistent tongue is a warning that something is wrong.

| Under Control | James 3:13-18 |

A controlled tongue comes from a wise heart.

    Worldly Wisdom

    Godly Wisdom

Life Principle: My words will reflect whatever or whoever hold my affections and loyalty.

The Bottom Line

In order to consistently speak wise and gracious words, we need to yield our hearts to the Holy Spirit's control.

Gracious Me!

Session 4
Speak: Lesson

James 3:2-18

If you've ever watched a reality competition show, then you've probably found yourself at some point talking to people on the show as if they could hear you through the television. During one episode of Survivor, every member of my family was shouting at the T.V., "Be quiet! Stop talking; just shut up!" But she didn't, and sure enough – one of our favorite players was voted off even though she was in no danger at all when they arrived at tribal council. I can identify – can't you? I've had words spill out of my mouth at the same time my brain was shouting, "Just stop talking!" Well, the Bible has a lot to say about what we say and how we say it. Let's see how James 3 can help us to become more gracious when we speak.

Main Thought: Words have consequences and reveal the true nature of the person speaking.

GIVING UP CONTROL
James 3:2-5a
A spiritually mature woman places her tongue under God's control.

More and more, people in our society say, post, and tweet whatever is on their minds with little thought given to the effect of their words. The ability to control what we say is a sign of spiritual maturity.[1] The word perfect in verse [2] can also be translated as mature (HCSB). Learning to exercise discipline over your tongue begins by asking, "Who is in control of my mouth?" James helps us answer this question with two illustrations.

First, a rider controls his horse by pulling back on the reins. The natural desire of the horse – to run free – is under the control of the one holding the reins. Likewise, our sin nature produces harsh, foolish, and slanderous words when it's allowed to run free. In order for the Holy Spirit to be in control of your tongue, you must choose to hand Him the reins day by day and moment by moment. By giving Him control of your mouth, you'll often sense Him pulling back, prompting you to stop talking or to just be quiet.

Next, a wise captain navigates his ship through dangerous waters and strong storms. What challenging circumstances are you currently trying to navigate? The pressures of life[2] can cause a sharp tongue unless God the Holy Spirit is at the wheel. The words you speak during life's most difficult moments may very well determine the course of your life or someone else's life.

When we speak ungracious words, it is usually caused by one of two things: 1) We're pushing our own agenda rather than focusing on God's purposes, or 2) we haven't properly placed our trust in God when life turns up the heat. In either case, we need to give control of our mouths to God if we want to be effective for His kingdom. What area of your speech do you need to surrender to God's control?

Life Principle: My words will not reflect God's grace unless I give Him control of my tongue.

DAMAGE CONTROL
James 3:5b-8
An uncontrolled tongue has the power to damage and destroy.

James gives two additional word pictures describing the damage words can cause. First, our tongue can sweep through like a wildfire and harm everyone in its path, unless it is restrained. Think for a moment about the characteristics of fire (burns, damages, spreads) and how those destructive features might show up in your speech.

Do you tend to lash out when the situation gets hot and you're angry? Scripture relates a quick temper to being foolish (Prov. 14:29). We all know that the old "sticks and stones" adage is false – words do hurt and cause damage, and the damage is hard to contain. Conflict and gossip can quickly spread through your family, church, and community, leaving behind broken relationships and crushed spirits. This week's daily study challenged us to use restraint by simply limiting what we say (Proverbs 10:19; 17:27-28). The thoughts and opinions we have when angry or upset are usually the ones we're the quickest to express.

Gracious Me!

I'm reminded of the damage fire can cause when I look at the set of china given to me by my mother-in-law. Some of the pieces were destroyed in a house fire when my husband was a child. We love to use the remaining pieces, even though they bear the dark marks of smoke damage from that night. Words can have the same lingering effect. Has your life been marked by destructive words, burned into your memory? If so, then be encouraged; you are valuable to God, just as that china still serves the purpose for which it was created. In fact, it is even more highly valued because of what it endured. Each time it's used, we express gratitude to the One who saved my husband and his family from the fire. Also, be aware of words you speak that can cause lasting damage. You can avoid causing hurt in another person's life by simply using restraint.

*"We all know how to be quiet,
but few of us know when."* - Anonymous

While an uncontrolled wildfire is destructive, a harnessed fire generates power and comfort. This week, your words could bring either comfort and encouragement or strife and destruction. When you submit your mouth to the control of the Holy Spirit, He provides grace so that you can voice thoughts that are used for God's purpose and God's glory.

Not only do unrestrained words damage and spread, they're also poisonous. The difference between poison and venom is interesting. Venom is usually injected under the skin by animals with fangs or stingers, whereas many poisonous animals have a self-defense mechanism that makes them deadly to touch,[3] eat, inhale, or swallow.[4] In this context, venomous words are those intended to land a blow, to sting. You may not be a person who walks around with your fangs showing, but what about when you're faced with a verbal attack? When our tongues go into self-defense mode, the things we say can be deadly to a relationship once digested by the listener. We can either give someone what we think they have coming, or we can extend God's grace.

Life Principle: Words spoken in the heat of the moment or in self-defense are seldom gracious.

QUALITY CONTROL
James 3:9-12
Praising God but then engaging in gossip, slander, or criticism is abnormal for a believer.

See if this scenario sounds familiar: you go to church, sing worship songs, and maybe even say, "Amen" during the sermon. Then at lunch – right after church – the conversation turns to rumors about another church member. Or maybe there's outright criticism of the worship leader or pastor. When you praise God and then tear someone down, your words reveal hypocrisy. That kind of inconsistency is as abnormal for a follower of Christ as fresh water and salt water coming from the same spring.

Colossians 4:6 says that our words should be full of grace, seasoned with salt. Salt is good, in measure. Don't miss this point – gracious words are intentional. Difficult conversations are sometimes necessary, but our words need to be chosen carefully. Just as salt heals and irritates at the same time, too much rebuke (or even too much cheer) is too much salt (Proverbs 25:20). Several years ago I asked my brother to teach me to surf. When I fell off the board, I gasped, swallowed a mouth full of salt water, and came up choking. Salt is an excellent seasoning but a poor fountain! Do your words go down like a cool spring, or are they choked down like salt water? Gracious words, like fresh water, give life and nourishment – they are refreshing (Proverbs 10:11).

James then points out that a tree can produce only one kind of fruit. Our speech should display the fruit of our resurrected nature rather than our old, sinful nature. Producing both kinds of fruit is unnatural and abnormal. Refreshing words have a source as surely as a freshwater spring has a source. You'll never consistently produce gracious words unless the Holy Spirit is your source.

> *The acts of the sinful nature are obvious: sexual immorality, impurity and debauchery; idolatry and witchcraft; hatred, discord, jealousy, fits of rage, selfish ambition, dissensions, factions and envy; drunkenness, orgies, and the like. I warn you, as I did before, that those who live*

> like this will not inherit the kingdom of God. But the fruit of the
> Spirit is love, joy, peace, patience, kindness, goodness, faithfulness,
> gentleness and self-control. Against such things there is no law. Those
> who belong to Christ Jesus have crucified the sinful nature with its
> passions and desires. – Galatians 5:19-24.

Life Principle: A hypocritical, inconsistent tongue is a warning that something is wrong.

UNDER CONTROL
James 3:13-18
A controlled tongue comes from a wise heart.

Did you notice in the daily study how many times Psalms and Proverbs connected what we say to either wisdom or foolishness? Well, here again in the book of James, we see a contrast between worldly wisdom and godly wisdom. Actually, there's no true wisdom when we display the traits of our old nature. We learned last week in Romans 6 how to live daily in the truth that our old nature has been crucified with Christ. If, however, you allow things like envy and selfishness to remain in your heart, then your words will likely come out as fire, poison, and salt water – words which reveal hypocrisy in the life of a believer. The key word in verse 14 is heart.

> [18]But the things that come out of the mouth come from the heart,
> and these make a man 'unclean'. [19]For out of the heart come evil
> thoughts, murder, adultery, sexual immorality, theft, false testimony,
> slander. – Matthew 15:18-19

Verse 19 reflects the natural state of our hearts unless a change takes place. When I was growing up, salvation was often referred to as "giving your heart to Jesus." That transfer of ownership should be reflected in how we talk. If you are a follower of Christ, then the Holy Spirit has taken up residence in your life. As you yield to His promptings, moment by moment, your heart will begin to produce His fruit – the fruit of the Spirit (Galatians 5:22-23). If Matthew 15:19 describes the heart in its natural state, then James 3:17-18 depicts a supernatural heart.

A heart full of godly wisdom laces our speech with words of peace, consideration, humility, mercy, impartiality, and sincerity. We give to others what God has given to us. When God is in control of our tongues, our words are like a comforting fire on a cold night and fresh water on a hot day. In short, our words are gracious.

On my 16th birthday, my parents gave me a heart necklace with a keyhole and a tiny key. My dad separated the key from the heart and kept it for himself. He said that he would give that key to the man I married. That night my dad took me on my first date and showed me how a gentleman behaved. He held the key to my heart until that kind of gentleman came along. Who holds the key to your heart? You will live to please that person – whether it is God, yourself, or someone else. If you claim loyalty to Christ, but your words are negative and biting, then either your heart doesn't truly belong to Christ, or you've yielded to your old nature rather than to the Holy Spirit.

Life Principle: My words will reflect whatever or whoever holds my affections and loyalty.

Think back on the things you've said this week and the way in which you said them. Close out this session by asking God to make you more aware of your words. This week, be careful to let your conversations be gracious, seasoned with salt, and pleasing to God. He will supply the grace to say the right thing at the right time and in the right way.

The Bottom Line

In order to consistently speak wise and gracious words, we need to yield our hearts to the Holy Spirit's control.

Gracious Me!

Session 5

Give

Session 5
Give: Daily Study

Main Thought: True generosity comes from grace, not from obligation.

DAY ONE: The Obstacle – Perspective

In order to handle finances graciously you have to view money and possessions from God's perspective. As a follower of Christ, your life isn't defined by what you own but by whom you are owned. Read Matthew 6:19-24 to see how Jesus challenges our perspective on material things.

1. In verses19-21 Jesus compares earthly and heavenly treasure. He defines treasure as whatever has captured one's heart. What do these verses teach about each kind of treasure?

2. What does Proverbs 23:4-5 say about earthly riches?

3. Using God-given skills and material things for His purpose and His glory result in storing up heavenly treasure. What are specific ways you can pursue heavenly treasure in the coming week? (1 Tim 6:17-19)

4. Materialism takes hold of your heart when things become your source of security or satisfaction. What do you learn from Ecclesiastes 5:10-20 about living for material gain?

The person who loves money…

The person who loves wealth…

The abundance of the rich…

The ability to enjoy work and wealth…

Matthew 6:22-23 shifts from what you love to how you think. What you choose to think about will determine what you have the most affection for. Being consumed with thoughts of gaining wealth is greed, whereas focusing your thoughts on serving God gives you the desire to use your resources for His purposes. Lastly, in verse 24 Jesus connects what you love and how you think to how you act. Here's an exercise that will help determine to whom or to what you are currently devoted.

   5. a. In the last week what occupied your thoughts, time and energy the most?

   b. Do a mental inventory of your bank and credit card statements; what do they reflect about who or what you love?

6. What insights do the following verses give regarding God's perspective on true wealth?

   Romans 11:33

   Ephesians 2:7

DAY TWO: The Promise - Provision

One main purpose of money is to provide what we need to live. Worry is the sin of not trusting God to provide. The only way to get rid of financial anxiety is to have confident dependence on God to meet every need. Read Matthew 6:25-33 and discover what Jesus said about priorities and provision.

1. Jesus told His disciples not to worry about food, clothing or what will happen tomorrow. What reasons does He give? Underline the reason that means the most to you in your present situation?

2. Pick out the phrase in verse 30 that's the opposite of trusting God.

3. Complete trust in God is demonstrated by allowing Him to set your priorities. What does verse 33 say a follower of Christ is to pursue first and what will be the result?

4. In what area of your life is God prompting you to seek first His kingdom and His righteousness? What will you have to stop pursuing in order to obey?

5. In the left column list some of what God has provided for you over and above your daily needs. On the right, itemize current needs that tempt you to worry. Spend a few moments thanking God for His provision (left column) and asking Him, in faith, to provide for your current needs (right column.)

God's Provision   Current Needs

DAY THREE: The Goal - Contentment

Yesterday's study pointed to God as the Provider of everything you have and need. The question that arises next is whether or not you are content with what God provides. Contentment is simply being satisfied with who you are and what you have. Today, we'll take a look at a few enemies of contentment and discover the secret to living a satisfied life.

1. 1 Timothy 6:6-11 is rich with insight on the subject of contentment. Paul reminds Timothy that the goals and expectations of a believer should be spiritual, not material. Which warnings from this passage is God using to get your attention regarding contentment?

(Check as many as apply)

☐ Contentment comes from God, not money or things (verse 6).

Session 5: Give

- ☐ Material things are temporary (verse 7).
- ☐ Don't confuse your needs with your wants (verse 8).
- ☐ Wanting to get rich is a trap that leads to foolish and harmful desires (verse 9).
- ☐ Desiring money can ruin a life rather than improve it (verse 9).
- ☐ Loving money is detrimental to spiritual growth (verse 10).

2. Paul told Timothy in verse 11 to flee from all this and pursue what, instead? Circle the word you need to pursue most in your current circumstances.

3. Read Philippians 4:10-13. What was Paul's secret of being content in any and every situation?

4. In Philippians 4:11-12 Paul said he has learned to be content, indicating that it was developed over time. What present situation is God using to teach you contentment?

5. What phrases in Philippians 3:7-11 show that Paul's satisfaction in life was not from material wealth but from his relationship with Christ?

6. What financial goals or expectations is God prompting you to change? How would it encourage more gracious giving in your life?

DAY FOUR: The Standard — Tithe

Tithing is part of the Mosaic Law given by God (Leviticus 27:30-33; Numbers 18:21-32; Deuteronomy 12:5-18.) It was the practice of bringing a tenth of their crops and herds to God as an acknowledgment, on Israel's part, that everything came from the Lord and belonged to Him. A portion of the tithe was given to Aaron and the Levites, whose occupation was serving in the tabernacle as God's priests. Today we'll look at tithing as the starting point of gracious giving.

1. According to Malachi 3:8-9, what problem had developed in Israel?

2. Malachi 3:10 is unique in that God invites His people to test Him regarding the tithe. What is the…

    Promise:

    Condition:

3. List how your tithes and offerings are used for God through your local church.

Session 5: Give

God adds an interesting detail in verses 11 and 12 regarding their productivity. God tells Israel that He will keep pests from destroying their crops and keep the fruit from falling off their vines. Their work will yield more productivity under His blessing. This is akin to what God did when their ancestors wandered in the desert for 40 years yet their clothes and shoes never wore out (Deuteronomy 29:5.) God is not only able to provide but also to sustain. Obedience in the matter of tithing allows God's children to go further on 90% with His blessing than on 100% without it.

But all of that was in the Old Testament under the Law. Does living under grace instead of the Law negate the principle of tithing? Let's find out what the New Testament says on the subject.

4. Both Jesus and Paul give added insight to being a faithful steward of all God has provided. What do you learn about tithing in the following passages?

   Matthew 23:23

   1 Corinthians 16:2

5. How have you experienced God's provision and sustaining power as a result of tithing?

DAY FIVE: The Challenge — Generosity

The Apostle Paul's writings say a lot about generosity and gracious giving. A major part of his third missionary journey was dedicated to collecting an offering from Gentile believers for persecuted Christians in Judea who were living in poverty. The church at Corinth quickly agreed to give to the cause, which influenced the Macedonian church to give a generous offering. A year later, however, the Corinthians had not followed through on their promise to give. Paul encourages the Corinthians to be openhanded. Prepare for today's study by reading 2 Corinthians 8.

1. Several principles about generosity can be taken from this passage. Use the verses listed to fill in the blanks, taking note of the principle given for each part.

    a. (Verse 1) The Macedonian church was given _____. God enables believers to be generous.

    b. (Verse 2) These believers gave out of their _____. Generosity isn't connected to outer circumstances.

    c. (Verses 3-5) The Macedonians gave _____ to God first then asked for the privilege to help God's people in need. Generosity should be the natural response for followers of Christ.

    d. (Verses 6-8) Paul encourages the Corinthians to _____ their act of grace and to _____ in this grace of giving. Being generous is a choice.

Session 5: Give

    e. (Verse 9) The grace shown to the believer by _____ is the motivation for generosity. Believers give graciously because Christ is gracious with them.

    f. (Verses 11-12) They were to give according to their _____. Generosity is connected to one's willingness, not the size of the gift.

2. Which of the above principles stands out to you most? Why?

Gracious Me!

Session 5
Give: Guide

Main Thought: True generosity comes from grace, not from obligation.

Instructions for Giving	2 Corinthians 9:6-7

The law of harvesting illustrates how God blesses authentic generosity.

> Give Generously

> Give Intentionally

> Give Cheerfully

Life Principle: My motivations and attitudes determine whether or not my gift is gracious.

The Source of Giving	2 Corinthians 9:8-11a

God graciously supplies all that's needed to sow and reap generously.

> God is Our Security

Session 5: Give

God is Our Supplier

Life Principle: Generosity comes through me, not from me.

The Results of Giving	2 Corinthians 11b-15

Generosity and obedience in giving results in thanks and praise to God.

    Thanks is Given

    Praise is Given

    Hearts are Connected

Life Principle: God can use an ungracious gift but He is robbed of praise and my faith isn't exercised.

The Bottom Line

A gracious woman recognizes that God's resources are for God's purposes.

Gracious Me!

Session 5
Give: Lesson

2 Corinthians 9:6-15

Early in our marriage we started keeping a journal of how God met many of our needs through the generosity of others. But as the years went by, I often neglected to do the same for the people God brought into my path, reasoning that I did not have the spiritual gift of giving (and I don't). Through this study, God revealed that I could, and should, grow in the grace of giving.

Day five of the daily study explored 2 Corinthians 8 and the offering from Gentile believers for the persecuted and impoverished Christians in Jerusalem. Paul urged the Corinthians to excel in the grace of giving because the Lord Jesus Christ had graciously given Himself for them. Today's session picks up with Paul's challenge to the Corinthians in chapter 9.

Main Thought: True generosity comes from grace, not from obligation.

INSTRUCTIONS FOR GIVING
2 Corinthians 9:6-7
The law of harvesting illustrates how God blesses authentic generosity.

Give Generously
It makes sense that a farmer's harvest is directly related to his planting. Picture a farmer walking over his field, reaching into his bag, and tossing a huge handful of seed. He cannot hold onto the seed if he wants to take in a plentiful harvest; he must be openhanded and scatter it generously. Now, relate that to being openhanded with your personal resources. We ask God to meet our needs, opening our hands to receive His blessings, but then often closing our fists around what He provides rather than being generous. Keep in mind that generosity doesn't look the same from person to person. Your situation is different from that of the person next to you.

It brings to mind a Mother's Day when my children were young. My eight-year-old daughter gave me two gifts of jewelry: a colorful plastic bracelet that had been given to her and a butterfly pin she made from small wooden craft pieces. She was openhanded with her personal treasure and her creative talents. Then my four-year-old son handed me a small box, wrapped in copy paper with a bow on top (the obvious work of my daughter). When I opened the box to find nothing inside, he said, "I filled it with kisses so you can have one whenever you want." Aw – right? He realized that he didn't have the same resources his sister had, so he was generous with himself. But don't miss this – she was generous with her time in helping him. Although their gifts were different, both were generous.

What does generosity look like in your present situation? Are you closed fisted with your time, talents, and treasure? Or are you willing to wholly offer yourself and all that you have to the Lord – for His purpose? Jesus taught the principle of generosity with a different illustration.

> *Give, and it will be given to you. A good measure, pressed down, shaken together and running over, will be poured into your lap. For with the measure you use, it will be measured to you. – Luke 6:38*

What we're willing to give up can often be measured with a teaspoon, while we request (and expect) blessings by the cup! Please don't misunderstand this verse as a formula for prosperity. We have to remember that not all sowing will result in reaping material blessings. God may choose to measure back in spiritual blessings such as wisdom, mercy, grace, and biblical truth.

> *Oh, the depth of the riches of the wisdom and knowledge of God! How unsearchable his judgments, and his paths beyond tracing out! - Romans 11:33*

> *But because of his great love for us, God, who is rich in mercy, made us alive with Christ even when we were dead in transgressions – it is by grace you have been saved. And God raised us up with Christ and seated us with him in the heavenly realms in Christ Jesus, in order that in the coming ages he might*

> *show the incomparable riches of his grace, expressed in his kindness to us in Christ Jesus.* - Ephesians 2:4-7

> *"Don't let the things money can buy rob you of things it can't."* - Anonymous

Give Decidedly

Paul also instructed the Corinthians to give intentionally. Spontaneous generosity is good, but because it's often based on emotion, it tends to be inconsistent. For instance, we all come across the bell ringers while shopping at Christmastime. You might give a little something each time you pass by or give one time but not the next. Or maybe pictures of hungry children and abused animals pull at your heartstrings, so you donate. All of those things are good. My point is this: once you give even the smallest amount, something in your psyche says, "I've done my part."

Giving a predetermined percentage or amount requires a commitment – a decision made in your heart (2 Corinthians 9:7). Last week we saw the connection between the heart and the mouth; this week the connection is between the heart and hands. God always gets around to whether the motives of our hearts please Him,[1] doesn't He? Since the things we say and do are directly related to the motives of our hearts, let's honestly evaluate our motives. Have you been generous with a family member in order to manipulate that person? Or perhaps your charitable giving is motivated by a desire to impress someone. Ask God to help you address any motives for giving that don't line up with His Word and His character.

Give Cheerfully

Your motives for giving will determine the attitude with which you give. Nothing exposes our motives and attitudes more quickly than money matters. Paul contrasts giving under compulsion with giving cheerfully. The word cheerful in verse 7 is from the Greek word *hilaros*,[2] from which we get the word hilarious, indicating laughter and happiness. It's the picture of obediently giving with a genuine smile on your face.

Years ago I heard a preacher tell the story of a preschooler who insisted on standing in her chair during dinner. The child and the parents soon became locked in a battle of the wills, but eventually they compelled her to sit down. The child blurted out, "I'm sitting on the outside, but I'm standing on the inside!" I've been there at times – outwardly obedient but inwardly rebellious. It's possible to be outwardly obedient to God in tithing or giving to a need, yet have a resentful attitude about handing over the gift. Gracious giving doesn't require coercion; it is a reasonable response to personally experiencing God's grace.[3]

If you're slow to be openhanded, then check whether your reluctance stems from insecurity, fear, or greed. If you feel pressure rather than joy in giving to your church, then search your heart to see if there's an area of ingratitude or rebellion to God. Learning to appreciate God's generosity to you makes it possible to give cheerfully – with a smile, literally.

Life Principle: My motivations and attitudes determine whether or not my gift is gracious.

THE SOURCE OF GIVING
2 Corinthians 9:8-11a
God graciously supplies all that is needed to sow and reap generously.

God is Our Security
The previous section briefly brought up the thought that a reluctance to give can be connected to financial fears and insecurities. Be assured that God will enable you to trust Him with your resources. He offers the grace we need to be openhanded. Paul didn't hesitate to use absolutes in verse 8 regarding God's ability to give exactly what is needed at exactly the right time.[4] He provides us all we need to do everything He has for us to do (Ephesians 2:10). Did you catch that last phrase? God always has sufficient funds for His work. If something seems to be tying up your resources (time, energy, material wealth), then take a closer look at whether you are engaged in God's will or your own agenda.

Is your security in God alone or in God plus something or someone else? Our insecurities are most often revealed during times of financial difficultly. Verse 9 is a quote from Psalm 112, which describes the unwavering trust that the righteous place in the Lord. They are compassionate and generous, even in the most challenging times. Dependency on God is a spiritual workout. The more you exercise your faith by trusting Him to supply every need and to give as He directs, the more your faith and character are strengthened.

I've faced sleepless nights at the sudden loss of employment, a lengthy medical crisis, and a large repair bill. Through each situation, we determined to tithe faithfully and trust in the Lord. Let's face it – that's hard! Time and again we experienced God's sufficiency firsthand. When my security is properly placed in God alone, I view my resources from His perspective; panic is replaced with inexplicable peace.

God is Our Supplier
When God prompts you to give, He either has already supplied or will supply the gift. Since God is the supplier and the multiplier (v10), there's no reason not to be generous. Gracious giving means that you trust God to do the math. He uses what we give to do what only He can do; the harvest is both tangible and eternal! Allowing God's resources to flow freely through your hands provides practical evidence of the righteous nature of Christ.[5]

You may be thinking, "Well, I tried giving to charity and tithing to my church, but I'm certainly not 'rich in every way'!" (v. 11a). We tend to compare our situations to people who have more than we do, rather than those who have less – don't we? What has God supplied that goes beyond your basic needs? Whatever you just thought of probably makes you rich by most world standards. And if you have access to a copy of God's Word, then you enjoy spiritual wealth too (Romans 11:33). Are you generous with your time and your knowledge of God? Will you ask God for the grace to exercise your faith by scattering the time, talents, and treasure that He has supplied to you?

Life Principle: Generosity comes through me, not from me.

THE RESULTS OF GIVING
2 Corinthians 9:11b-15
Generosity and obedience in giving will result in thanks and praise to God.

Thanks is Given
We usually offer expressions of gratitude when someone goes out of his or her way on our behalf. Paul offers the Corinthians a paradigm shift. As the Supplier of both the gift and the grace to give, God would receive the thanks for their generosity.

Who is giving thanks to the Lord because of your generosity? Tithing to your local church provides the funds needed to operate week by week, and additional offerings make it possible to do ministry, not only in your community but also around the world. Additionally, non-profit organizations rely on donations to fund medical research or supply basic needs to impoverished people. We hear more and more about the misspending of charitable funds, which feeds a growing cynicism regarding giving. Still, credible organizations and genuine needs are out there. Somewhere right now, a pastor, researcher, or aid worker is praying for God to supply the funds to continue their work. True, the nature of charitable giving reduces your chances of receiving a thank-you note, but your generosity is the answer to someone's prayer, resulting in thanks to God.

Praise is Given
Whereas thanksgiving is about the recipient being grateful, praise indicates exalting the Lord because of Who He is. Our generosity reflects on our heavenly Father in the same way that parents are praised for a child's good behavior and character. Your obedience in giving is cause for someone else to turn to the Lord in worship. Shouldn't our confession of faith in Jesus Christ as Lord equal obedience to Him in giving? We often stop short by simply praying for God to meet someone's needs when He may want us to be part of the answer to that prayer. What recent prayer request is the Holy Spirit prompting you to act upon? Doing nothing may very well rob God of praise.

Hearts are Connected

Nothing fosters affection more than when someone cares about you enough to make a financial sacrifice. My husband was pastoring a small church when our first child was born. We both felt that God was leading me to quit my job and be a full-time mother during that season of life. We started receiving a check every month from a couple who knew our finances were tight. They lived on a modest income, so the gift was a sacrifice on their part (they had four kids of their own!) Their check faithfully arrived in our mailbox for years. To no one's surprise, that same couple didn't hesitate to offer their time as well – again, at great personal sacrifice. They were the answer to our prayers for God's provision, and in turn we prayed for them. Their generosity is like a cord that has connected our lives and hearts through the decades. I don't know if either of them has the spiritual gift of giving, but they certainly exhibited the grace of giving.

Verse 15 closes out this amazing chapter by offering thanks to God for His indescribable gift. Words are inadequate to describe what God has given us in Jesus.

> *"You and I are saved because God believed in grace giving."[6] - Warren Wiersbe*

Life Principle: God can use an ungracious gift, but He's robbed of praise, and my faith isn't exercised.

Each of our sessions stresses the idea that being gracious is freely giving what God has graciously given to us. How can we keep from being generous with our time, talents, and treasure if that is in the forefront of our minds? How would you categorize your present giving – reluctant or cheerful? Are you willing to ask God how He wants to use the resources at your disposal this week?

Bottom Line

A gracious woman recognizes that God's resources are for God's purposes.

Gracious Me!

Session 6

Forgive

Session 6
Forgive: Daily Study

Main Thought: A gracious woman forgives as freely as God has forgiven her.

DAY ONE: A Question

We discovered in session one that we'd much rather live under grace than under law. Being gracious means we don't hold others to an impossible standard of perfection even though personal hurt and disappointments are inevitable. Today, we'll begin looking at the issue of forgiveness from Matthew 18:21-22 and answer the question, "How many times should I forgive?"

1. Rabbis and scribes taught that forgiving an offense three times was sufficient.[1] How many times did Peter suggest in his question to Jesus? Why do you think he chose that number?

2. What was Jesus' answer? What point do you think He was trying to make?

3. Nehemiah 9 contains a lengthy prayer, chronicling God's faithfulness despite Israel's history of disobedience.

    a. What are some of the sins Israel confessed to God?

    b. List the character traits and descriptions of God you find in this chapter.

Gracious Me!

    c. How does Israel's history with God relate to how Jesus answered Peter in Matthew 18:22?

    d. Name specific ways you can live out God's model of forgiveness found in Nehemiah 9:17.

DAY TWO: A Merciful King

Yesterday, we looked at Peter's question to Jesus regarding how many times to forgive. Today, we'll examine Jesus' response in a parable about mercy and forgiveness from Matthew 18:23-35. A parable is an earthly story meant to illustrate a spiritual truth. In this story, we understand the king to represent God, the servants to represent Christians, and debt to symbolize sin.

    1. In Roman currency, a denarii was a common day's wage. A talent was worth 6,000 denarii.[2] How much was the impossible debt the servant owed the king? How many denarii (or days of work) did that equal?

    2. List the responses from verses 25-27. For each response, decide if it's an example of the Law, justice or mercy.

        a. The King's order

        b. The servant's plea

c. The King's decision

3. According to Ephesians 2:8, how was your sin debt paid? Does this reflect the Law, justice or mercy?

4. Put yourself in the story as the servant with God as the King and the debt as your sin. What spiritual conclusions can you draw from verses 23-27?

DAY THREE: A Choice
God's forgiveness shouldn't just be a fact of the Christian life but a realization that shows up in how we respond when hurt by others. Our ability to forgive should have nothing to do with the amount of hurt we experience. Today, we'll see that any wrong done towards us is small compared to our offense against God and that accepting mercy but refusing to give it is ungracious. Read Matthew 18:28-30.

1. How much did the fellow servant owe the forgiven servant? How many days' wages does that equal?

2. What similarities and differences do you see between verses 23-27 and verses 28-30?

Similarities	Differences

3. What similarities and differences can you think of between your offenses toward God and others' offenses against you? What about God's response to you and your response to others?

4. Why should the servant have forgiven his fellow servant's debt, according to the king? See verses 32-33. How does this answer Peter's question from verse 21?

5. The servant walked straight from receiving grace and mercy in the presence of the king and showed no compassion for his fellow servant. What has God, your King, shown or given you in your personal quiet time this week that should be reflected in how you treat others?

6. The forgiven servant had every legal right to put his fellow servant in prison for his debt. Likewise, the hurts we experience are real. However, when we internalize God's grace, we care more about the other person than their offense toward us. Without mentioning a name, what offense will you choose to

forgive as a reflection of God's forgiveness toward you?

DAY FOUR: The Consequences

God may let you suffer the consequences of an unforgiving heart. Holding a grudge torments you more than the person who hurt you. Today's study picks up where we left off yesterday in Matthew 18 and dives into the consequences of choosing not to forgive. Read verses 34-35.

1. What was the result of the servant's unwillingness to forgive? What warning did Jesus give at the end of the parable?

2. Was the ending to this parable evidence that one can lose their salvation? Use any Scripture you choose to support your answer. Any of the following passages will be helpful: Romans 8:35-39; 2 Corinthians 1:22; Hebrews 7:25; Hebrews 9:26-28; Titus 3:3-7; 1 Peter 1:5; Eph. 1:13.

Refusing to show mercy harmed the fellowship with the master and the fellow servant. We will look more at this aspect in tomorrow's study.

3. What does it mean to forgive from the heart (v35)? How do you know if you've forgiven from the heart? Psalm 103:8-12; Isaiah 43:25

DAY FIVE: Forgiveness and Prayer

Intimacy with God, through prayer, is a vital part of a believer's sanctification. When our horizontal relationships with family, friends, co-workers or neighbors are skewed due to an unforgiving heart, our vertical relationship with God is also affected. We conclude our study this week by seeing how Jesus connected forgiveness and prayer.

1. Read The Model Prayer from Matthew 6:9-13. Put verse 12 in your own words. From what you learned in yesterday's study, what do you think Jesus meant by debt?

2. According to Matthew 6:14-15, what is the benefit of forgiving others? What is the consequence of not forgiving?

3. How regularly do you include the forgiveness of others in your prayer life?

    Never   Always

    1   2   3   4   5   6   7   8   9   10

4. How does refusing to forgive someone harm your intimacy with the heavenly Father? What's the difference between your relationship with God and your fellowship with Him?

5. What connection do you make between Mark 11:25 and Luke 6:28?

6. What issue of forgiveness is standing between you and the heavenly Father? Of whom do you need to ask forgiveness?

Session 6
Forgive: Guide

Main Thought: Genuine forgiveness is found in the new self not the old self.

Forgiven in Christ	Ephesians 4:22-5:2

Just as the old self was forgiven because of Christ, the new self forgives in Christ.

    An Act of Grace

    Put Off the Old

    Put On the New

Life Principle: *I extend God's love and grace when I choose to forgive.*

Session 6: Forgive

| Hidden in Christ | Colossians 3:3-14 |

Forgiveness comes by being hidden and dressed in Christ.

How Are You Bearing Up?

Take Off the Old

Put On the New

Life Principle: I need to get dressed spiritually each day.

The Bottom Line

A gracious woman forgives as freely as God has forgiven her.

Session 6
Forgive: Lesson

Ephesians 4:22-5:2 and Colossians 3:3-14

We learned in session four how to put our tongues under God's control and avoid hurting others with the words we use. But what about when others injure us by what they say? How should we respond when we're affected by their actions or inactions? Some offenses, such as lying, unfaithfulness, and gossip, can be hard to forgive. Yet God tells us that it's not only possible for believers to forgive completely – it's expected!

Main Thought: A gracious woman forgives as freely as God has forgiven her.

FORGIVEN IN CHRIST
Ephesians 4:22-32
Just as the old self was forgiven because of Christ, the new self forgives in Christ.

An Act of Grace
Since we are to forgive just as God forgave us in Christ (v. 32), then we need to think deeply for a moment about God's forgiveness. God's holy and divine nature forgives sin on the basis of Christ's sacrifice alone. In order for the demands of the Law to be met, blood had to be shed. God's love is unfathomable, but forgiveness of sin is ultimately an act of grace. The word "forgiving" in verse 32 literally means being gracious.[3] Forgiving wrongs, however, isn't an ability people are born with. Just watch a group of small children at play – their inherent selfishness will eventually show up. Like those children, my selfish, prideful nature has often gotten in the way of forgiving another person the same way God forgave me – freely. Can you identify? Forgiveness is a selfless act of humility. To truly understand how to graciously forgive, we need to put verse 32 into context with what Paul wrote earlier in the chapter, so let's back up and start with verse 22.

Session 6: Forgive

Put Off the Old

Before Paul encouraged the Ephesians to forgive as they had been forgiven, he urged them to put off their old self: the sinful nature that was a slave to sin. Think about it. Why would followers of Christ ever want to go back to their old way of life? We now have a choice – we don't have to act according to our old nature; however, we need a new attitude of mind (v. 23).

> *Those who live according to the sinful nature have their minds set on what that nature desires; but those who live in accordance with the Spirit have their minds set on what the Spirit desires. The mind of sinful man is death, but the mind controlled by the Spirit is life and peace. The sinful mind is hostile to God. It does not submit to God's law, nor can it do so. Those controlled by the sinful nature cannot please God. You, however, are controlled not by the sinful nature but by the Spirit, if the Spirit of God lives in you. And if anyone does not have the Spirit of Christ, he does not belong to Christ.*
> – Romans 8:5-9

Your mindset is determined by which nature you live to please, and you'll live to please the nature on which your mind is set. We choose which nature we obey. One nature pleases our flesh and seeks a personal agenda, while the other pleases God and desires His purposes. Ephesians 4:25-31 is a description of the mindset of the old self, which eventually leads to being an angry and bitter person. If bitterness takes root in your heart, then it will eventually affect your entire being and everyone in your path – not just the one you're angry with.

An article from CNN Health describes the effects bitterness can have on the human body. The article's sources state that people who are chronically angry and bitter have higher blood pressure and heart rate, putting them at higher risk for heart disease as well as other conditions. Hormones in the body change with strong feelings of anger. The article states, "The data that negative mental states cause heart problems is just stupendous. The data is just as established as smoking, and the size of the effect is the same."[4] And, the Mayo Clinic reports that choosing forgiveness by letting go of grudges and bitterness can lead to greater psychological well-being, less anxiety, lower blood pressure, fewer symptoms of depression, and lower risk of alcohol and substance abuse.[5] Time and distance from a hurt can diminish animosity, but only genuine forgiveness removes bitterness.

Put on the New
When the old self is discarded, we're free to put on the new self, characterized by kindness and compassion (Ephesians 4:24, 32). Putting on the nature of Christ gives you the ability to love supernaturally, which leads to forgiveness.

Take a look at Ephesians 5:1-2. Two characteristics of children show up in these verses: 1) Children imitate their parents, and 2) Children are loved by their parents. Have you watched a young girl try to imitate her mother by walking in her high-heeled shoes? Like that child, we should imitate our heavenly Father and live a life of love because we are loved. How much are you loved? So much that Christ willingly gave Himself up for you! Love should be characteristic of Christ's followers because we share in the divine nature through the indwelling of the Holy Spirit, giving us the ability to love as He loves (1 John 4:8-11). Forgiveness is the natural response of godly love (1 Peter 4:8).

> *And hope does not disappoint us, because God has poured out his love into our hearts by the Holy Spirit, whom he has given us. - Romans 5:5*

> "*The Holy Spirit reveals that God loved me not because I was lovable, but because it was His nature to do so. Now, He says to me, show the same love to others –*
>
> *'Love as I have loved you.' [God] will bring any number of people about you whom you cannot respect, and you must exhibit [His] love to them as [He] has exhibited it to you.*" – Oswald Chambers

Who do you have a hard time forgiving? You don't have to like someone to love that person as God loves and to extend His grace. You might be able to dismiss the hurts of people you don't particularly care for, but the people you love the most can cut you to the core. When those hurts come, we often build brick walls around our hearts for future protection. Opening your heart to God's love opens your hearts to His forgiveness. The person who has hurt or offended you may not deserve your love and forgiveness any more than you and I deserved God's love and forgiveness. Will you be gracious and forgive him or her anyway?

Life Principle: I extend God's grace and love when I choose to forgive.

HIDDEN IN CHRIST
Colossians 3:3-14
Forgiveness comes by being hidden and dressed in Christ.

How Are You Bearing Up?
Paul uses a thought-provoking phrase in verse 13: Bear with each other. The word bear comes from forbear, which means to be patient when wronged or provoked.[6] It implies the need to forgive over and over again or to deal with something over a period of time. This idea ties in to Peter's question from the daily study: "How many times should I forgive?" Before we address that though, we need to look at another noteworthy word in verse 13: grievance. It's feeling that you've been treated unfairly, having a [just] reason for complaining or being unhappy with a situation.[7]

Paul encourages the Colossians, as well as us, to live in a spirit of forgiveness. This kind of mindset is patient when provoked and gracious when treated unfairly. Let's narrow down the application of verse 13 to the people with whom we live, work, and worship. You've probably already thought of a continuing situation where your patience is wearing thin. What would it look like to forebear graciously in that situation? I'm not suggesting that you become anyone's doormat, but Paul urges us to remember why we are to forgive the faults of others – because the Lord has forgiven us. Living in the same household or working in the same space with imperfect human beings necessitates putting up with their flaws and imperfections – just as they do ours!

A special word to parents – let your kids hear you ask for each other's forgiveness. Too many times we let a moment of irritation show in front of our kids, but we fail to teach them how to humbly resolve conflict by our example. Just as we did in Ephesians, putting verse 13 into context shows us how to bear with one another and live in a spirit of forgiveness. Let's go back to the beginning of Colossians 3 and reread verses 3-9.

Take Off the Old

Paul essentially said the same thing to the Colossians that he said to the Ephesians – since you died in Christ to your old self, don't live according to your old nature. We're good at rationalizing why our old self acts out: "This is just the way I am" or "God made me this way." Remember – anything not resembling the characteristics of Christ should be taken off, not excused. Will you determine to place those traits under the control of the Holy Spirit? For instance, a tendency to be stubborn becomes strength of conviction and godly resolve in the Spirit. Literally, that old person is hidden behind the Person of Jesus Christ!

Put on the New

With the old self taken off, we can choose to put on the characteristics of Christ (vv. 10-14); just as we physically take off old clothes and put new ones on. How would your day improve if you went through the mental exercise of putting off your old self with your pajamas and putting on the new self as you got dressed? Release thoughts and attitudes related to lust, greed, anger, or slander. Choose instead to live the day clothed in compassion, kindness, humility, gentleness, and patience.

After you're dressed, don't forget to accessorize! Put on love, like a belt that holds together perfectly the other traits of your new nature in Christ. Start the day by saying, "Today, I will choose to respond in love, even to the most difficult or irritating person." Thinking through getting dressed spiritually may seem silly, but it can serve as a useful reminder at the start of the day – to be hidden in Christ and to love and forgive as He loves and forgives you.

Life Principle: I need to get dressed spiritually each day.

"I can forgive anything except…." How would you finish that statement now that you've studied God's perspective on forgiveness? Before we can offer genuine love and forgiveness, we first need to come to grips with the depths of God's love and forgiveness toward us (Luke 7:47). I remember a conversation with one of those wise, gracious women I so want to be like – my mom. She said, "Love is the fountain from which forgiveness flows." This week, will your old self respond by withholding mercy, or will you put on the nature of Christ and extend an act of grace?

Bottom Line

Genuine forgiveness is found in the new self, not the old.

Epilogue

It seems like a lifetime since I first prayed, "Lord, help me to be a more gracious woman." Looking back, it's amazing to see how much God has grown me and stretched me. He's taught me to open my heart and my hands as a conduit of His grace. Yet, if I've learned anything at all it's that becoming more gracious is a life-long pursuit. Studying what it means to be gracious has made me more aware of when I'm in danger of hoarding God's grace rather than allowing it to flow to others.

I pray that you have a new realization of how gracious God has been, and continues to be, in your life. Since His grace is continually available to us, then it should continually flow through us. Will you accept the challenge to be a conduit through whom His grace can grow and flow? It starts by maintaining a right relationship with the Lord. At the outset of this study I encouraged you to set a time and place to spend at least 15 minutes a day in God's Word and in prayer. Please don't slip out of that habit now. As you open Scripture, look for what you can learn about the character and nature of God. Ask, "How should I respond to what I've learned?" Then confess any sinful attitudes the Spirit reveals. Remember, His grace has moved us from death to life and allows us to stand before Him free of guilt and shame. Ask the Lord to help you grow in the godly character qualities you discover - just as you've become more gracious in response to His grace.

Yes, God's grace is freely available but that doesn't mean we'll automatically be gracious. Extending grace to the people around us is a choice and growing in grace is a process. A seed doesn't become a mature plant in a day or a week, but over time with proper care. You'll grow a little more each day as you learn to die to your own desires and choose to live for God's desires. He's already provided everything you need to live a godly and gracious life.

We studied three practical ways to extend God's grace: speaking, giving, and forgiving. Which one did you identify as a current strength? In which one do you have the most room for growth? Really take some time to think back through those lessons. First, reflect on the things you've said over the last week. Our words reveal a lot about us. It's impossible for your speech to be a display of God's grace unless you've first given Him control of your tongue. The first step to consistently speaking wise and gracious words is yielding your heart to the Holy Spirit's control; listening for when He prompts you to stay quiet or to speak. God's Spirit leads us to say the right thing at the right time and in the right way.

Next, examine whether your motivations and attitudes toward giving are aligned with Scripture. Biblical giving encompasses generosity with our entire being - our time, talents, and treasure. Personally, studying gracious giving has changed my relationship with money. Although I've always been frugal, I misplaced my security in the provision rather than in the Provider. Recognizing that God has a purpose for the resources He provides has helped me to properly place my security in Him, to be content with what He's provided, and to be a more generous person. Learning to open my hands and give freely has exercised my faith like never before. I'd like to say that I'm completely free of financial anxiety, but I'm still growing in the grace of giving. How about you? Do you tend to open your hands to receive what God provides but then close your fist around it? Ask God to help you grow in His grace, allowing His generosity toward you to flow to someone else.

Finally, consider whether you're withholding forgiveness from someone. Of the three areas we've studied, forgiveness is the most difficult to measure. Our words can be heard and read; our generosity can be seen in tangible ways; but we can hide an unforgiving spirit - for a little while. Too often we allow emotions to determine the outcome of a disagreement or a hurtful situation. Yet, God's forgiveness toward us is seen so clearly in the gift of salvation. We extend God's love and grace when we choose to forgive as freely as God has forgiven us. That kind of forgiveness is impossible if we're operating in our old nature. Remember to start each day by getting dressed spiritually; taking off the old person and putting on the new nature you have in Christ Jesus.

So, are you gracious? Would your family, friends, and co-workers say that you're a conduit of God's grace or would they describe you as a grace hoarder? I'll make you a promise. If you'll commit to really dig into God's Word each day and learn how He has been and continues to be gracious to you, then He will meet you there. Your time alone with the Lord will become the most treasured part of your day. I'm praying for you! "Lord, help us to be more gracious women."

Endnotes

Lesson 1: Grace

[1] Randy Alcorn, *The Grace and Truth Paradox* (Sisters: Multnomah Publishers, Inc., 2003), 32; 35.

[2] John Phillips, *Exploring the Epistle of James: An Expository Commentary* (Grand Rapids: Kregel Publications, a division of Kregel, Inc., 2004), 135.

[3] John F. Walvoord and Roy B. Zuck, eds., *The Bible Knowledge Commentary: New Testament* (USA: SP Publications, Inc., 1983), 878.

[4] *Ibid*, 866.

Lesson 2: Worship

[1] *Life Application Bible* (Wheaton: Tyndale House Publishers, Inc., 1991), 2121

[2] *Ibid*.

[3] *Ibid*.

[4] John F. Walvoord and Roy B. Zuck, eds., *The Bible Knowledge Commentary: Old Testament* (USA: SP Publications, Inc., 1983), 173-183.

[5] John Phillips, *Exploring Hebrews* (Grand Rapids: Kregel Publications, a division of Kregel, Inc., 1977, 1988), 121.

[6] John F. Walvoord and Roy B. Zuck, eds., *The Bible Knowledge Commentary: New Testament* (USA: SP Publications, Inc., 1983), 803.

[7] W.A. Criswell and Paige Patterson, eds., *The Believer's Study Bible* (Nashville: Thomas Nelson Publishers, 1991), 1748-1749.

[8] W.E. Vine, Merrill F. Unger, and William White, Jr., eds., *Vine's Expository Dictionary of Biblical Words* (Nashville: Thomas Nelson Publishers, 1985), 535.

[9] Criswell and Patterson, eds., 1603.

[10] *Ibid*, 1609.

Lesson 3: Choose

[1] Oswald Chambers, *My Utmost for His Highest* (USA: Dodd, Mead & Co, Inc., 1935), 264.

[2] Warren W. Wiersbe, *The Bible Exposition Commentary – Volume 1* (USA: SP Publications, 1989), 531.

3 *Ibid.*, 532.

4 *Ibid.*

5 Selwyn Hughes, *Every Day Light* (Nashville: Broadman & Holman Publishers, 1997), 289.

6 Wiersbe, 533.

Lesson 4: Speak
1 John F. Walvoord and Roy B. Zuck, eds., *The Bible Knowledge Commentary: New Testament* (USA: SP Publications, Inc., 1983), 827.
2 Warren W. Wiersbe, *The Bible Exposition Commentary - Volume 2* (SP Publications, 1989), 358.
3 "Poison dart frog." *New World Encyclopedia*, 4 April 2008. Web 12 April 2012. newworldencyclopedia.org/p/index.php?title=Poison_dart_frog&oldid=687374
4 "Difference Between Venom and Poison." Koshal, 5 Nov. 2014. 12 April 2012. differencebetween.com/difference-between-venom-and-vs-poison/

Lesson 5: Give
1 Warren W. Wiersbe, *The Bible Exposition Commentary – Volume 1* (USA: SP Publications, 1989), 660.
2 W.A. Criswell and Paige Patterson, eds., *The Believer's Study Bible* (Nashville: Thomas Nelson Publishers, 1991), 1658.
3 Wiersbe, 660.
4 *Ibid.*, 661.
5 John F. Walvoord and Roy B. Zuck, eds., *The Bible Knowledge Commentary: New Testament* (USA: SP Publications, Inc., 1983), 575.
6 Wiersbe, 663.

Lesson 6: Forgive
1 Warren W. Wiersbe, The Bible Exposition Commentary: Volume 1 (USA: SP Publications, 1989), 67.
2 W.A. Criswell and Paige Patterson, eds., The Believer's Study Bible (Nashville: Thomas Nelson Publishers, 1991), 1369.
3 John F. Walvoord and Roy B. Zuck, eds., The Bible Knowledge Commentary: New Testament (Zondervan Bible Publishers, 1983), 637.
4 "Blaming others can ruin your health." CNN Health. Cable News Network, 18 Aug. 2011. Web 24 Sept. 2016. cnn.com/2011/HEALTH/08/17/bitter.resentful.ep/index.html

5 "Forgiveness: Letting go of grudges and bitterness." Mayo Foundation for Medical Education and Research. 23 Nov. 2011. Web 24 Sept. 2016. <http://www.mayoclinic.org/healthy-lifestyle/adulthealth/ in-depth/forgiveness/art-20047692
6 W.E. Vine, Merrill F. Unger, and William White, Jr., eds., Vine's Expository Dictionary of Biblical Words (Nashville: Thomas Nelson Publishers, 1985), 247.
7 "Grievance." Merriam-Webster.com. Merriam-Webster, n.d. Web. 24 Sept. 2016.

www.ingramcontent.com/pod-product-compliance
Lightning Source LLC
Chambersburg PA
CBHW070647050426
42451CB00008B/308